D1396776

Steak houses today are as strong as ever. The reason: They know how to deliver a truly great piece of beef. And now that the secret's out, you'll be delighted to discover how easy it is to re-create those great flavors at home. A.1. Steak Sauce salutes the resurgence of the steak house! With our zesty marinades, sauces and rubs, you'll find it's simple to deliver the sizzle along with the steak in your own kitchen.

This seal assures you that every recipe in *A.1.® Steak House Favorites* has been tested in the *Better Homes and Gardens®* Test Kitchen. This means that each recipe is practical and reliable, and meets high standards of taste appeal.

© Copyright 1998 Nabisco, Inc.
© Copyright 1998 Meredith Corporation. All Rights Reserved.
Produced by Meredith Integrated Marketing, 1716 Locust Street, Des Moines, Iowa 50309-3023. Printed in Hong Kong.
Printing number and year: 5 4 3 2 1  03 02 01 00 99
Library of Congress Catalog Card Number 98-67675
ISBN: 0-696-20951-9 Canadian BN 12348 2887 RT.

The *Better Homes and Gardens®* Test Kitchen Seal is a registered trademark of Meredith Corporation.

"A.1.," "Grey Poupon," "Oreo," and "Planters" are registered trademarks of Nabisco Brands Company.

"TABASCO®" is a registered trademark and service mark of McIlhenny Company, Avery Island, LA 70513.

# A.1. Steak House
## FAVORITES

**PICTURED ON COVER: SIRLOIN STEAK PROVENÇALE AND HERB BUTTERED MUSHROOMS (RECIPES, PAGES 38 AND 78)**

# APPETIZERS

To launch a festive mood,
lead off the meal with one
of these tried-and-true steak
house appetizers. Whether it's
a taste of seafood or a hearty
soup you crave, you'll find
irresistible recipes that taste
great and are easy to make.

BEER-BOILED SHRIMP WITH
COCKTAIL SAUCE
(RECIPE, PAGE 4)
LOUISIANA CRAB CAKES
(RECIPE, PAGE 5)

# Beer-Boiled Shrimp with Cocktail Sauce

**MAKES 8 SERVINGS • PREP TIME: 25 MINUTES**
**COOK TIME: 8 MINUTES • CHILL TIME: 1 HOUR**

*Recipe is pictured on pages 2 and 3.*

1 (12-fluid ounce) bottle beer
4 cups water
2 pounds raw shrimp, shelled, leaving
     tails intact and deveined
1½ cups ketchup

2 tablespoons prepared horseradish
1 tablespoon Worcestershire sauce
2 teaspoons fresh lemon juice
1 teaspoon TABASCO® Pepper Sauce

❶ Heat beer and water in heavy large pot to a boil. Add shrimp. Simmer, uncovered, for 1 to 3 minutes or until shrimp turn pink, stirring occasionally. Drain shrimp and rinse with cold water. Chill until serving time.

❷ Mix ketchup, horseradish, Worcestershire, lemon juice and pepper sauce in bowl. Cover; refrigerate at least 1 hour to blend flavors.

❸ Serve shrimp with sauce.

# Cheddar-Stuffed Mushrooms

**MAKES 24 APPETIZERS • PREP TIME: 15 MINUTES**
**COOK TIME: 8 MINUTES**

24 large fresh mushrooms, about
     2 inches in diameter, cleaned
¼ cup sliced green onions
1 clove garlic, finely chopped
½ to ¾ teaspoon TABASCO®
     Pepper Sauce

¼ cup margarine *or* butter
⅔ cup fine dry bread crumbs
½ cup shredded cheddar cheese
     (about 2 ounces)

❶ Remove stems from mushrooms; reserve caps. Chop enough stems to make 1 cup. Cook and stir chopped stems, green onions, garlic and pepper sauce in margarine or butter in large skillet over medium-high heat until tender. Remove from heat; stir in bread crumbs and cheese.

❷ Spoon crumb mixture into mushroom caps. Place caps on a 15½x10½x1-inch baking pan.

❸ Bake at 425°F for 8 to 10 minutes or until heated through.

# Louisiana Crab Cakes

**MAKES 10 APPETIZERS • PREP TIME: 30 MINUTES**
**CHILL TIME: 1 HOUR • COOK TIME: 12 MINUTES**

*Recipe is pictured on pages 2 and 3.*

| | |
|---|---|
| 1 pound fresh crabmeat, cleaned and flaked | 1 teaspoon dry mustard |
| ½ cup finely chopped green bell pepper | ½ teaspoon TABASCO® Pepper Sauce |
| ¼ cup finely chopped onion | ¾ cup plain dry bread crumbs, divided |
| 1 egg, beaten | Vegetable oil |
| | Leaf lettuce |

❶ Mix crabmeat, pepper, onion, egg, mustard, pepper sauce and ½ cup bread crumbs. Cover; refrigerate for 1 hour or until mixture firms up.

❷ Shape crab mixture into 10 (¾-inch-thick) patties; coat with remaining crumbs.

❸ Pour oil into heavy large skillet to ½-inch depth; heat over medium heat. Brown crab cakes, in batches, for 3 to 5 minutes on each side or until done. Drain on paper towels. Arrange crab cakes on a lettuce-lined platter. Serve warm.

## CLEANING CRABMEAT

*Fresh cooked or canned crabmeat can contain some cartilage or even bits of shell. You will want to remove it before using the crabmeat. To remove the cartilage, simply use a fork to pick through the crabmeat. Lift out any cartilage and shell and discard it. If you'd like to flake the crabmeat for a mixture such as crab cakes, use the fork to gently break up large chunks.*

# Potato Leek Soup

MAKES 4 SERVINGS • PREP TIME: 10 MINUTES
COOK TIME: 20 MINUTES

½ cup sliced leeks

1 tablespoon margarine *or* butter

2 medium potatoes (12 ounces), cleaned, peeled and sliced

1¼ cups chicken broth

1¼ cups half-and-half *or* light cream

❶ Cook and stir leeks in spread in saucepan over medium heat 5 minutes or until tender. Stir in potatoes and broth; heat to a boil. Reduce heat; cover and simmer 12 to 15 minutes or until tender.

❷ Remove from heat; cool slightly. Blend potato mixture in electric blender or food processor until smooth.

❸ Combine half-and-half or light cream and potato mixture in same saucepan; heat through. Serve warm or refrigerate and serve cold.

# Clams in Coquille Shells

MAKES 2 SERVINGS • PREP TIME: 15 MINUTES
COOK TIME: 10 MINUTES

⅓ cup chopped celery

2 tablespoons margarine or butter, melted and divided

1 tablespoon all-purpose flour

⅓ cup half-and-half *or* light cream

¼ to ½ teaspoon TABASCO® Pepper Sauce

1 (6½-ounce) can minced clams, drained

¾ cup soft bread crumbs (about 1 slice bread), divided

2 tablespoons snipped parsley, divided

❶ Cook celery in 1 tablespoon margarine or butter for 5 minutes or until tender. Stir in flour until smooth. Gradually stir in half-and-half or light cream and pepper sauce; cook, stirring until mixture thickens and boils. Stir in clams, half of the crumbs and 1 tablespoon parsley.

❷ Spoon mixture into 2 greased coquille shells (individual baking shells) or two 6-ounce custard cups. Toss remaining crumbs, parsley and spread; sprinkle over clam mixture.

❸ Bake at 400°F about 10 minutes or until browned.

# Lobster Bisque

3 green onions, sliced
and divided
2 tablespoons margarine *or* butter
¼ cup all-purpose flour
1½ cups milk
6 ounces cubed, cooked lobster; crabmeat, drained and flaked; frozen,
peeled, cooked shrimp *or* lobster-
flavored chunk-style fish pieces

1½ cups half-and-half *or* light cream
¼ cup dry sherry *or* milk
¼ teaspoon salt
Dash ground white pepper

❶ Reserve 2 tablespoons sliced green onion tops for garnish. Cook and stir remaining green onions in margarine or butter in medium saucepan over medium heat for 1 minute.

❷ Stir in flour until smooth. Gradually stir in milk; cook, stirring until mixture thickens and boils. Cook and stir 1 minute more.

❸ Add seafood, half-and-half or light cream, sherry or milk, salt and white pepper. Cook and stir until heated through. To serve, ladle soup into bowls. Garnish with reserved green onion tops.

### LOBSTER OR SURIMI?

*For cooked lobster meat, steam a fresh or frozen tail until the flesh turns opaque, then cool and chop. Or, use the more economical product called chunk-style fish pieces or surimi (made from cod with lobster flavoring). Although surimi is not shellfish, the flavor and texture are similar, and you don't have to shell and chop.*

MANHATTAN CLAM CHOWDER

# Manhattan Clam Chowder

**MAKES 8 SERVINGS • PREP TIME: 15 MINUTES**
**COOK TIME: 20 MINUTES**

1 pint shucked clams *or*
   two (6½-ounce)
   cans minced clams
Water
1 cup clam-tomato juice cocktail
2 medium potatoes (12 ounces),
   cleaned and chopped

1 cup chopped green *or*
   red bell pepper
¼ cup sliced green onions
¼ teaspoon ground black pepper
1 (14½-ounce) can diced
   tomatoes with basil,
   garlic and oregano, undrained

❶ Chop clams, reserving juice; set clams aside. Strain clam juice to remove bits of shell. (Or, drain canned clams, reserving juice.) Measure juice; add enough water to equal 1½ cups liquid.

❷ Combine clam juice mixture, clam-tomato juice cocktail, potatoes, bell pepper, green onions and black pepper in large saucepan; heat to a boil. Reduce heat; cover and simmer about 15 minutes or until potatoes are just tender.

❸ Stir in undrained tomatoes and clams; heat through.

## SHUCKED CLAM POINTERS

*Select shucked clams that are plump, have clear juices and are without any pieces of shell. Refrigerate the clams with their juices for up to 3 days. If there aren't enough juices to cover the clams, mix 1 cup water and ½ teaspoon salt. Pour enough of this mixture over the clams to cover them. If you want to store the clams longer, freeze them with their juices for up to 6 months.*

# French Onion Soup

MAKES 6 SERVINGS • PREP TIME: 15 MINUTES
COOK TIME: 25 MINUTES

1 pound onions, thinly sliced
3 tablespoons margarine *or* butter
2 (14½-ounce) cans beef broth
1 teaspoon Worcestershire sauce

Dash ground black pepper
6 slices French bread, toasted
⅔ cup shredded Swiss cheese
(about 3 ounces)

❶ Cook and stir onions in margarine or butter in covered large saucepan over medium heat for 20 minutes. Stir in beef broth, Worcestershire sauce and pepper; heat to a boil. Remove from heat.

❷ Place bread on baking sheet; sprinkle bread with cheese. Broil 4 to 5 inches from heat about 1 minute or until cheese is melted and golden.

❸ Ladle soup into bowls; top with bread slices.

## BEEF BROTH

*When a recipe calls for beef broth, you can always use homemade, but these days, who has time? Instead, choose canned ready-to-use broth. You can choose from regular or lower-sodium varieties.*

# Zippy Potato Skins

MAKES 6 SERVINGS • PREP TIME: 15 MINUTES
COOK TIME: 70 MINUTES

6 large baking potatoes
(3½ to 4 pounds)
¼ cup margarine *or* butter
½ teaspoon chili powder
¼ to ½ teaspoon TABASCO®
Pepper Sauce

⅓ cup finely chopped Canadian bacon
*or* 6 slices bacon, cooked
and crumbled
¼ cup sliced green onions
1½ cups shredded Monterey Jack *or*
cheddar cheese (6 ounces)

❶ Thoroughly scrub potatoes; pat dry. Prick each potato with a fork. Bake at 400°F for 1 hour or until tender.

❷ Mix margarine or butter, chili powder and pepper sauce; set aside.

❸ Cut each potato in half lengthwise. Scoop out the inside of each potato half, leaving a ¼-inch-thick shell. (Cover and chill the leftover potato pulp for another use.) Cut each potato shell lengthwise into thirds. Place potato skin strips on baking sheet. Broil 3 to 4 inches from heat for 5 minutes. Brush with margarine or butter mixture. Sprinkle with bacon, green onions and cheese. Broil about 1 minute or until cheese melts.

# Hot Artichoke Dip

MAKES 1½ CUPS • PREP TIME: 15 MINUTES
COOK TIME: 30 MINUTES

1 (14-ounce) can artichoke hearts,
drained and chopped
½ cup grated Parmesan cheese

½ cup mayonnaise *or* salad dressing
2 green onions, finely chopped
1 teaspoon TABASCO® Pepper Sauce

❶ Mix all ingredients in medium bowl. Spread in shallow 1-quart baking dish or 9-inch pie plate.

❷ Bake, uncovered, at 375°F for 20 to 30 minutes or until bubbly around edges. Serve hot as a dip with crackers.

# STEAKS
## RIBS AND MORE

Why do people beat a path to the door of a favorite steak house? The answer's clear: great steaks. Now you can re-create the same choice flavors at home with trusted recipes for the classics, plus new inspirations, too. For extra flavor, take advantage of these zesty marinades, pastes, bastes, rubs and sauces. Another bonus: delicious new ideas for beef ribs, kabobs and burgers.

CHATEAUBRIAND WITH
A.1. BÉARNAISE SAUCE
(RECIPE, PAGE 14)

# Chateaubriand with A.1. Béarnaise Sauce

**MAKES 8 SERVINGS • PREP TIME: 10 MINUTES**
**ROAST TIME: 35 MINUTES • STAND TIME: 15 MINUTES**
**COOK TIME: 20 MINUTES**

*Recipe is pictured on pages 12 and 13 and on back cover.*

1 (2-pound) beef tenderloin roast
½ cup A.1. ORIGINAL Steak
    Sauce, divided
1¼ pounds small new potatoes, cleaned
    and peeled around the center
12 tablespoons margarine *or*
    butter, divided
2 tablespoons finely chopped parsley

Salt and ground black pepper, to taste
2 tablespoons chopped shallots *or*
    green onions
1 egg yolk
2 teaspoons snipped fresh tarragon
    leaves *or* ¾ teaspoon dried
    tarragon, crumbled

❶ Place roast on rack in shallow roasting pan; brush with 2 tablespoons steak sauce. Roast at 425°F for 35 to 45 minutes or until internal temperature of roast reaches 140°F for medium rare or 155°F for medium, brushing with 2 tablespoons steak sauce about halfway through roasting. Remove from oven. Cover with foil; let stand 15 minutes (internal temperature will rise 5°F).

❷ Heat potatoes and enough water to cover to a boil. Reduce heat; cover and simmer for 15 to 20 minutes or until tender. Drain. Toss potatoes with 4 table-spoons margarine or butter and parsley until margarine or butter melts. Season with salt and pepper. Cover; keep warm.

❸ Mix remaining steak sauce and shallots or green onions in top of double boiler. Place double boiler top over double boiler bottom containing simmering water (upper pan should not touch water). Cook and stir for 3 to 5 minutes or until mixture thickens. Stir in 2 tablespoons margarine or butter until melted. Remove top of double boiler from heat; whisk in egg yolk and tarragon. Place double boiler top over double boiler bottom containing simmering water; cook and stir until mixture starts to thicken. Add remaining margarine or butter, 2 tablespoons at a time, whisking until smooth after each addition. Remove from heat. Cover; keep warm. Slice roast; serve with sauce and potatoes.

# Steaks with French Onion Sauce

**MAKES 4 SERVINGS • PREP TIME: 15 MINUTES**
**COOK TIME: 6 MINUTES**

1 small onion, sliced and separated
    into rings
1 tablespoon vegetable oil
¼ cup beef broth

¼ cup A.1. SWEET & TANGY
    Steak Sauce
2 (8-ounce) boneless beef rib-eye
    steaks, ¾ inch thick

❶ Cook and stir onion in oil in skillet over medium heat for 5 minutes or until tender.

❷ Stir in broth and steak sauce. Heat to a boil; keep warm.

❸ Grill or broil steaks for 3 to 5 minutes on each side or until desired doneness.
Serve steaks with warm onion sauce.

# Zesty Onion Porterhouse Steaks

**MAKES 4 SERVINGS • PREP TIME: 10 MINUTES**
**MARINATE TIME: 1 HOUR • COOK TIME: 14 MINUTES**

½ cup A.1. ORIGINAL Steak Sauce
½ cup bottled Thousand Island
    salad dressing

1 (1.2-ounce) envelope dry onion
    soup mix
2 (1-pound) beef loin porterhouse
    steaks, 1 inch thick

❶ Mix steak sauce, salad dressing and soup mix in bowl. Place steaks in nonmetal
dish or plastic bag; add steak sauce mixture, turning to coat both sides. Cover;
refrigerate for 1 hour, turning steaks occasionally.

❷ Remove steaks from marinade; place marinade in small saucepan. Add water to
marinade to thin sauce to desired consistency. Heat to a boil. Reduce heat; simmer
for 5 minutes.

❸ Grill or broil steaks for 7 to 9 minutes on each side or until desired doneness.
Serve steaks with warm onion sauce.

# Sirloin Steak with Red Onion Relish

**MAKES 6 SERVINGS • PREP TIME: 10 MINUTES**
**COOK TIME: 17 MINUTES**

¼ to ½ teaspoon coarse ground
  black pepper
1 (1½-pound) boneless beef top
  sirloin steak, ¾ inch thick
3 teaspoons vegetable oil, divided

1 large red onion, thinly sliced and
  separated into rings
¼ cup A.1. ORIGINAL Steak Sauce
½ teaspoon dried sage, crumbled

❶ Sprinkle pepper onto both sides of steak, pressing into steak.

❷ Cook steak in 2 teaspoons oil in large nonstick skillet over medium heat for
5 minutes on each side or until desired doneness. Remove from skillet; keep warm.

❸ Add remaining oil to drippings in skillet. Cook and stir onion in skillet over
medium heat about 5 minutes or until tender-crisp.

❹ Stir in steak sauce and sage; cook for 2 minutes. Serve over steak.

## THROUGH THICK AND THIN

*The thickness of steak affects the cooking time, whether you're grilling, broiling or pan-broiling. It makes sense that the thicker the steak, the longer it will take to cook in the center. It's a good idea to measure the thickness of steak before cooking, so you can cook it exactly to the stage of doneness you like. For medium rare, the meat should be slightly red at the center, with the juices still a little red.*

*For medium, the meat should be slightly pink. For medium well, the pink should be very faint. For well done, the meat should be brown throughout and the juices clear.*

**SIRLOIN STEAK WITH RED ONION RELISH AND CHEESY
TWICE-BAKED POTATOES (RECIPE, PAGE 81)**

# T-Bone Steaks with Bacon-Mushroom Sauce

**MAKES 4 SERVINGS • PREP TIME: 25 MINUTES**
**COOK TIME: 14 MINUTES**

5 slices bacon, cut into ¼-inch pieces (about 4 ounces)

1 (8-ounce) package fresh mushrooms, sliced (about 3 cups)

¾ cup A.1. ORIGINAL Steak Sauce

¼ cup dry sherry *or* water

1 teaspoon packed brown sugar

2 (1-pound) beef loin T-bone steaks, 1 inch thick

❶ Cook bacon in large skillet over medium heat until crisp. Remove bacon, reserving 2 tablespoons drippings in skillet. Drain bacon on paper towels.

❷ Cook and stir mushrooms in drippings for 5 minutes or until tender.

❸ Stir in steak sauce, dry sherry or water, brown sugar and cooked bacon; heat to a boil. Reduce heat; simmer for 5 minutes. Keep sauce warm.

❹ Grill or broil steaks for 7 to 9 minutes on each side or until desired doneness. Serve with warm mushroom sauce.

## CUTTING-BOARD SAFETY

*Plastic versus wood? Both types of cutting boards are safe to use with meat. However, do not use the same board for raw and cooked meat without cleaning it first. Scrub cutting boards thoroughly with hot, soapy water after each use. Discard cutting boards with deep nicks or grooves that could harbor bacteria.*

# T-Bone Steaks with Chunky Tomato Sauce

**MAKES 4 SERVINGS • PREP TIME: 20 MINUTES**
**COOK TIME: 14 MINUTES**

2 cups sliced onions
2 tablespoons olive oil
1 (8-ounce) can peeled tomatoes,
    drained and chopped

½ cup A.1. BOLD & SPICY *or*
    A.1. ORIGINAL Steak Sauce,
    divided
¼ cup chopped parsley
2 (1-pound) beef loin T-bone steaks,
    1 inch thick

❶ Cook and stir onions in oil in skillet over medium heat for 5 minutes or until tender.

❷ Stir in tomatoes and ¼ cup steak sauce; heat to a boil. Reduce heat; simmer for 5 minutes. Remove from heat; stir in parsley. Keep warm.

❸ Grill or broil steaks for 7 to 9 minutes on each side or until desired doneness, brushing with remaining steak sauce. Serve steaks with warm tomato sauce.

### CUTTING STEAK INTO PORTIONS

*A standard serving of meat should be the same size as a*

*deck of cards. But steak is made for celebrating, so on*

*special occasions, it's fine to provide a few extra bites.*

*A 4- to 6-ounce portion satisfies most steak lovers.*

# Steak Diane

¼ cup finely chopped shallots
2 tablespoons olive oil, divided
2 (8-ounce) boneless beef top
    loin steaks, ¾ inch thick

½ cup A.1. BOLD & SPICY or
    A.1. ORIGINAL Steak Sauce
1 tablespoon capers, drained
1 clove garlic, finely chopped
1 tablespoon finely chopped parsley

❶ Cook and stir shallots in 1 tablespoon oil in skillet over medium heat for about 5 minutes or until tender.

❷ Increase heat to high; add remaining oil to skillet. Add steaks; cook for 2 minutes on each side.

❸ Stir in steak sauce, capers and garlic; heat to a boil. Reduce heat; simmer for 3 minutes or until steaks are desired doneness. Stir in parsley. Add a little water, if necessary, to thin sauce.

## COOKING TENDER CUTS

*Quick-cooking methods, such as grilling and broiling, call for the tenderest cuts of beef. You can often interchange these cuts in recipes. To grill or broil, choose top loin (also called strip or shell), sirloin, T-bone (a combination of the top loin and tenderloin), Porterhouse (a similar but larger combination cut) or tenderloin steaks.*

STEAK DIANE

# Beef Tenderloins with Red Wine Sauce

**MAKES 4 SERVINGS • PREP TIME: 10 MINUTES**
**COOK TIME: 18 MINUTES**

½ teaspoon coarse ground black pepper
4 (4-ounce) beef tenderloin steaks,
    1 inch thick
1 tablespoon vegetable oil

¼ cup chopped onion
¼ cup A.1. ORIGINAL Steak Sauce
¼ cup dry red wine
1 teaspoon dried marjoram, crumbled

❶ Sprinkle pepper onto both sides of steaks, pressing into steaks.

❷ Cook steaks in oil in skillet over medium heat for 5 minutes on each side or until desired doneness. Remove from skillet; keep warm.

❸ Cook and stir onion in skillet over medium-high heat for 3 to 4 minutes or until tender.

❹ Stir in steak sauce, wine and marjoram; heat to a boil. Reduce heat; simmer for 2 minutes or until about ⅓ cup sauce remains. Serve warm wine sauce over steaks.

# Beef Tenderloins with Roasted Garlic Sauce

**MAKES 4 SERVINGS • PREP TIME: 20 MINUTES**
**COOK TIME: 12 MINUTES**

1 whole garlic bulb, separated but not
    peeled (10 to 12 cloves)
¾ cup A.1. ORIGINAL *or*
    A.1. BOLD & SPICY Steak
    Sauce, divided

¼ cup dry red wine *or* water
¼ cup finely chopped onion
4 (4-ounce) beef tenderloin steaks,
    1 inch thick

❶ Place unpeeled garlic on baking sheet. Bake at 500°F for 10 to 15 minutes or until soft; cool. Squeeze pulp from skins; chop slightly.

❷ Combine garlic pulp, ½ cup steak sauce, wine or water and onion in small saucepan; heat to a boil. Reduce heat; simmer for 5 minutes. Keep warm.

❸ Grill or broil steaks for 6 to 8 minutes on each side or until desired doneness, brushing occasionally with remaining steak sauce. Serve steaks with warm garlic sauce.

# Grilled Steak with Blue Cheese Sauce

**MAKES 6 SERVINGS • PREP TIME: 15 MINUTES**
**COOK TIME: 8 MINUTES**

¾ cup crumbled blue cheese
    (3 ounces), divided
½ cup heavy cream
½ cup A.1. BOLD & SPICY *or*
    A.1. ORIGINAL Steak Sauce,
    divided

1 tablespoon all-purpose flour
1 (1½-pound) boneless beef top round
    steak, ¾ inch thick
¼ cup sliced green onions

❶ Combine ½ cup blue cheese, heavy cream, 6 tablespoons steak sauce and flour in small saucepan. Cook and stir over medium heat until cheese melts and mixture begins to boil. Keep warm.

❷ Grill or broil steak for 4 to 6 minutes on each side or until desired doneness, brushing occasionally with remaining steak sauce.

❸ Slice steak; serve topped with warm blue cheese sauce, remaining blue cheese and green onions.

**NOTE:** Blue cheese goes by many names, such as Stilton, Gorgonzola or Maytag.

### JUDGING THE COAL TEMPERATURE

*Coals are ready when most of them are ash-gray;
glowing red coals are too hot and black coals are too cool.
To test the temperature, place your hand, palm side down,
near the grill rack. If you can hold it there 2 seconds, the
coal temperature is hot; 3 seconds means medium-hot;
4 seconds, medium and 5, medium-low.*

# Beef Tenderloins with Cream Sauce

**MAKES 4 SERVINGS • PREP TIME: 5 MINUTES**
**COOK TIME: 15 MINUTES**

4 (4-ounce) beef tenderloin steaks,
 ¾ inch thick
1 tablespoon margarine *or* butter
½ cup dairy sour cream
¼ cup A.1. ORIGINAL Steak Sauce

¼ cup milk
2 teaspoons all-purpose flour
2 teaspoons snipped fresh thyme
 leaves *or* ½ teaspoon dried
 thyme, crumbled

❶ Cook steaks in hot margarine or butter in skillet over medium heat for 5 minutes on each side or until desired doneness. Remove from skillet and keep warm.

❷ Combine sour cream, steak sauce, milk, flour and thyme in same skillet.

❸ Cook and stir over medium-high heat until mixture bubbles. Reduce heat; simmer for 1 minute. Serve with steaks.

**NOTE:** Steak house chefs sear tenderloins with special equipment. Home cooks can best capture that unique look and flavor by using a well-heated, heavy skillet.

### COOKING WITH SOUR CREAM

*Sour cream cooked too fast over high heat can curdle. To prevent this, mix the sour cream with flour and other ingredients before warming, so its temperature can rise gradually.*

BEEF TENDERLOINS WITH CREAM SAUCE

# Rib-Eye Steaks with Horseradish Sauce

**MAKES 4 SERVINGS • PREP TIME: 10 MINUTES**
**COOK TIME: 6 MINUTES**

4 ounces light cream cheese
  (Neufchâtel), softened
½ cup A.1. ORIGINAL or
  A.1. BOLD & SPICY Steak
  Sauce, divided

2 tablespoons milk
2 tablespoons prepared horseradish
2 tablespoons chopped green onion
2 (8-ounce) boneless beef rib-eye
  steaks, ¾ inch thick

❶ Mix cream cheese, ¼ cup steak sauce, milk and horseradish in bowl; stir in green onion. Cover; refrigerate until serving time.

❷ Grill or broil steaks for 3 to 5 minutes on each side or until desired doneness. Serve steaks with horseradish sauce.

# Steak au Poivre

**MAKES 6 SERVINGS • PREP TIME: 10 MINUTES**
**COOK TIME: 10 MINUTES**

1 (1½-pound) beef top sirloin steak,
  ¾ inch thick
½ cup A.1. ORIGINAL Steak
  Sauce, divided

2 teaspoons cracked black pepper
½ cup dairy sour cream
2 tablespoons ketchup

❶ Brush both sides of steak with 2 tablespoons steak sauce; sprinkle pepper onto both sides of steak, pressing firmly into steak. Set aside.

❷ Combine remaining steak sauce, sour cream and ketchup in medium saucepan. Cook and stir over low heat until heated through (do not boil); keep warm.

❸ Grill or broil steak for 5 to 7 minutes on each side or until desired doneness. Serve steak with warm sour cream sauce.

# Individual Beef Wellingtons

**MAKES 4 SERVINGS • PREP TIME: 35 MINUTES**
**COOK TIME: 25 MINUTES • STAND TIME: 5 MINUTES**

4 tablespoons A.1. SWEET &
TANGY Steak Sauce, divided
4 tablespoons deli *or* canned
mushroom *or* liver pâté *or*
one (4-ounce) can mushrooms,
drained and chopped
½ teaspoon dried marjoram, crumbled
½ teaspoon ground black pepper

¼ teaspoon salt
4 (4-ounce) beef tenderloin steaks,
1 inch thick
1 (17½-ounce) package frozen puff
pastry (2 sheets), thawed
1 egg white, beaten
½ cup prepared beef gravy

❶ Stir 1 tablespoon steak sauce into pâté or mushrooms; set aside.

❷ Brush each steak with ¾ teaspoon steak sauce. Mix marjoram, pepper and salt; sprinkle onto both sides of steaks, pressing into steaks. Spread 1 tablespoon pâté or mushroom mixture on top of each steak.

❸ Cut each thawed pastry sheet into 2 portions. Place each steak (pâté or mushroom side down) on center of a pastry piece. Wrap pastry around meat, trimming excess pastry; moisten and seal ends.

❹ Place filled pastries, seam side down, in a greased shallow baking pan. Brush pastry with beaten egg white. Re-roll pastry trimmings to make decorative cutouts, if desired; place on pastries. Brush again with egg white.

❺ Bake at 425°F for 25 minutes or until pastry is golden and internal temperature of steak reaches 140°F for medium rare or 155°F for medium. Let stand 5 minutes (internal temperature will rise 5°F during standing).

❻ Heat remaining steak sauce and prepared beef gravy until hot. Serve with steaks.

# Sliced Steak with Bold Pepper Sauce

MAKES 6 SERVINGS • PREP TIME: 15 MINUTES
COOK TIME: 8 MINUTES

1 cup thinly sliced red bell pepper
1 cup thinly sliced green bell pepper
2 tablespoons olive oil

¾ cup A.1. BOLD & SPICY or
     A.1. ORIGINAL Steak Sauce
1 tablespoon dry sherry or water
1 (1½-pound) boneless beef top round
     steak, ¾ inch thick

❶ Cook and stir peppers in oil in skillet over medium-high heat for 5 minutes or until tender-crisp.

❷ Stir in steak sauce and sherry or water; heat to a boil. Reduce heat; simmer for 5 minutes. Keep warm.

❸ Grill or broil steak for 4 to 6 minutes on each side or until desired doneness. Slice steak and serve with warm pepper sauce.

### BROILING BEEF

*Broiling is a favorite way to cook tender beef because, with a minimum of time and fuss, the high heat creates the crisp crust and juicy interior that steak lovers cherish. Position the rack so the food on the broiler-pan rack will be 3 to 5 inches from the heat (closer for thin steaks, farther for thick cuts), then preheat the broiler. After half of the broiling time, flip the steaks.*

SLICED STEAK WITH BOLD PEPPER SAUCE

# Chili-Beer Glazed Steaks

**MAKES 8 SERVINGS • PREP TIME: 15 MINUTES**
**COOK TIME: 12 MINUTES**

⅔ cup A.1. ORIGINAL or
    A.1. BOLD & SPICY
    Steak Sauce
⅔ cup chili sauce

½ cup beer
½ cup sliced green onions
4 (8-ounce) boneless beef top loin
    steaks, 1 inch thick

❶ Combine steak sauce, chili sauce, beer and green onions in small saucepan; heat to a boil. Reduce heat; simmer for 5 minutes. Keep warm.

❷ Grill or broil steaks for 6 to 8 minutes on each side or until desired doneness, brushing occasionally with ¼ cup steak sauce mixture.

❸ Serve steaks with remaining warm chili-beer sauce.

# Beer-Braised Brisket

**MAKES 8 SERVINGS • PREP TIME: 15 MINUTES**
**COOK TIME: 2½ HOURS**

1 (4½-pound) beef brisket, trimmed
1 (12-fluid ounce) bottle ale *or* beer
¾ cup A.1. SWEET & TANGY
    Steak Sauce
1 medium red onion, chopped

1 tablespoon packed brown sugar
1½ teaspoons dried thyme, crumbled
2 tablespoons cornstarch dissolved
    in 2 tablespoons cold water

❶ Place meat in large roasting pan. Mix ale or beer, steak sauce, onion, brown sugar and thyme; pour over meat. Cover pan with foil.

❷ Bake at 350°F for 2½ to 3 hours or until fork tender. Remove brisket; set aside.

❸ Skim fat from cooking liquid and place in small saucepan. Heat to a boil; stir in cornstarch mixture. Cook and stir until mixture thickens and begins to boil. Slice brisket and serve with warm sauce.

**CHILI-BEER GLAZED STEAKS**

BASIL BEEF

# Basil Beef

**MAKES 6 SERVINGS • PREP TIME: 10 MINUTES**
**MARINATE TIME: 30 MINUTES • COOK TIME: 8 MINUTES**

⅓ cup A.1. BOLD & SPICY Steak Sauce
   Grated peel and juice from 1 lime
1 tablespoon finely chopped garlic
1 tablespoon dried basil, crumbled

2 teaspoons dried mint, crumbled
2 teaspoons ground ginger
1 (1½-pound) boneless beef top
   round steak, ¾ inch thick

❶ Mix steak sauce, lime peel and juice, garlic, basil, mint and ginger. Place steak in nonmetal dish or plastic bag; add steak sauce mixture, turning to coat both sides. Cover; refrigerate for 30 minutes.

❷ Remove steak from marinade; discard marinade. Grill or broil steak for 4 to 6 minutes on each side or until desired doneness.

# Garlic Steak

2 tablespoons finely chopped garlic
1 (1½-pound) boneless beef top
  sirloin steak, ¾ inch thick

½ cup A.1. ORIGINAL Steak Sauce

❶ Spread garlic onto both sides of steak, pressing into steak. Place steak in nonmetal dish or plastic bag; add steak sauce, turning to coat both sides. Cover; refrigerate for 30 minutes.

❷ Remove steak from marinade; discard marinade. Grill or broil steak for 5 to 7 minutes on each side or until desired doneness.

# Zesty Italian Steak

1 (0.6-ounce) envelope zesty Italian
  salad dressing mix
1 (1½-pound) boneless beef top round
  steak, ¾ inch thick

½ cup A.1. ORIGINAL or
  A.1. BOLD & SPICY
  Steak Sauce

❶ Sprinkle salad dressing mix onto both sides of steak, pressing into steak. Place steak in nonmetal dish or plastic bag; add steak sauce, turning to coat both sides. Cover; refrigerate for 30 minutes.

❷ Remove steak from marinade; discard marinade. Grill or broil steak for 4 to 6 minutes on each side or until desired doneness.

# Spicy Citrus Steak

**MAKES 6 SERVINGS • PREP TIME: 10 MINUTES**
**MARINATE TIME: 30 MINUTES • COOK TIME: 8 MINUTES**

1 tablespoon grated lemon peel

1 tablespoon grated orange peel

1 (1½-pound) boneless beef top round steak, ¾ inch thick

½ cup A.1. BOLD & SPICY Steak Sauce

❶ Spread citrus peels onto both sides of steak, pressing into steak. Place steak in nonmetal dish or plastic bag; add steak sauce, turning to coat both sides. Cover; refrigerate for 30 minutes.

❷ Remove steak from marinade; discard marinade. Grill or broil steak for 4 to 6 minutes on each side or until desired doneness.

# A.1. Quick Seasoned Steak

**MAKES 6 SERVINGS • PREP TIME: 5 MINUTES**
**MARINATE TIME: 30 MINUTES • COOK TIME: 8 MINUTES**

1 to 3 teaspoons coarse ground black pepper

1 teaspoon seasoned salt

1 (1½-pound) boneless beef top round steak, ¾ inch thick

½ cup A.1. ORIGINAL Steak Sauce

❶ Sprinkle pepper and salt onto both sides of steak, pressing into steak. Place steak in nonmetal dish or plastic bag; add steak sauce, turning to coat both sides. Cover; refrigerate for 30 minutes.

❷ Remove steak from marinade; discard marinade. Grill or broil steak for 4 to 6 minutes on each side or until desired doneness.

# Garlic and Cracked Pepper Steak

**MAKES 6 SERVINGS • PREP TIME: 8 MINUTES**
**MARINATE TIME: 1 HOUR • COOK TIME: 8 MINUTES**

¼ cup A.1. ORIGINAL Steak Sauce

1 tablespoon vegetable oil

1 teaspoon cracked black pepper

2 cloves garlic, finely chopped

1 (1½-pound) boneless beef top round steak, ¾ inch thick

❶ Mix steak sauce, oil, pepper and garlic in bowl. Place steak in nonmetal dish or plastic bag; add steak sauce mixture, turning to coat both sides. Cover; refrigerate for 1 hour, turning occasionally.

❷ Remove steak from marinade; discard marinade. Grill or broil steak for 4 to 6 minutes on each side or until desired doneness.

# Italian Seasoned Steak

**MAKES 6 SERVINGS • PREP TIME: 5 MINUTES**
**MARINATE TIME: 1 HOUR • COOK TIME: 8 MINUTES**

⅓ cup A.1. ORIGINAL Steak Sauce

2 teaspoons Italian seasoning

1 teaspoon garlic powder

1 (1½-pound) boneless beef top round steak, ¾ inch thick

❶ Mix steak sauce, Italian seasoning and garlic powder in bowl. Place steak in nonmetal dish or plastic bag; add steak sauce mixture, turning to coat both sides. Cover; refrigerate for 1 hour, turning steak occasionally.

❷ Remove steak from marinade; discard marinade. Grill or broil steak for 4 to 6 minutes on each side or until desired doneness.

**NOTE:** Crush the Italian seasoning between your fingers to release more flavor.

# Zesty Lemon Steak

**MAKES 6 SERVINGS • PREP TIME: 5 MINUTES**
**MARINATE TIME: 1 HOUR • COOK TIME: 8 MINUTES**

¼ cup A.1. SWEET & TANGY
    Steak Sauce
¼ cup lemon juice

1 (1½-pound) boneless beef top round
    steak, ¾ inch thick

❶ Mix steak sauce and lemon juice in bowl. Place steak in nonmetal dish or plastic bag; add steak sauce mixture, turning to coat both sides. Cover; refrigerate for 1 hour, turning steak occasionally.

❷ Remove steak from marinade; discard marinade. Grill or broil steak for 4 to 6 minutes on each side or until desired doneness.

# Lemon-Ginger Steak

**MAKES 8 SERVINGS • PREP TIME: 10 MINUTES**
**MARINATE TIME: 4 HOURS • COOK TIME: 16 MINUTES**

⅓ cup A.1. ORIGINAL Steak Sauce
¼ cup bourbon *or* apple juice
¼ cup lemon juice
2 tablespoons vegetable oil
1 clove garlic, finely chopped

1 teaspoon ground ginger
½ teaspoon coarse ground black pepper
1 (2-pound) beef top sirloin steak,
    1 inch thick

❶ Mix steak sauce, bourbon or apple juice, lemon juice, oil, garlic, ginger and pepper in bowl. Place steak in nonmetal dish or plastic bag; add steak sauce mixture, turning to coat both sides. Cover; refrigerate 4 to 24 hours, turning steak occasionally.

❷ Remove steak from marinade; discard marinade. Grill or broil steak for 8 to 10 minutes on each side or until desired doneness.

# Sirloin Steak Provençale

**MAKES 6 SERVINGS • PREP TIME: 10 MINUTES**
**MARINATE TIME: 1 HOUR • COOK TIME: 10 MINUTES**

⅓ cup A.1. ORIGINAL Steak Sauce
3 green onions, finely chopped
2 tablespoons snipped fresh rosemary
  *or* 2 teaspoons dried rosemary,
  crumbled

1 tablespoon grated lemon peel
1 tablespoon finely chopped garlic
2 teaspoons dried thyme leaves,
  crumbled
1 (1½-pound) boneless beef top
  sirloin steak, ¾ inch thick

❶ Mix steak sauce, green onions, rosemary, lemon peel, garlic and thyme in bowl. Place steak in nonmetal dish or plastic bag; add steak sauce mixture, turning to coat both sides. Cover; refrigerate for 1 hour, turning steak occasionally.

❷ Remove steak from marinade; discard marinade. Grill or broil steak for 5 to 7 minutes on each side or until desired doneness.

**NOTE:** If you're using fresh rosemary, toss additional sprigs on the coals to scent the meat.

---

### MARINATING MADE EASY

*A plastic bag takes the mess out of marinating. Mix the ingredients and coat the meat right in the bag. Seal the bag tightly so it won't leak when you turn the meat; odors won't escape either. And cleanup is speedy— just throw the bag away.*

**SIRLOIN STEAK PROVENÇALE AND HERB-BUTTERED MUSHROOMS**

(RECIPE, PAGE 78)

# Argentinian London Broil

MAKES 6 SERVINGS • PREP TIME: 10 MINUTES
MARINATE TIME: 1 HOUR • COOK TIME: 8 MINUTES

½ cup finely chopped onion
⅓ cup A.1. BOLD & SPICY Steak Sauce
1 tablespoon finely chopped garlic

4 teaspoons dried oregano, crumbled
1 (1½-pound) boneless beef top round
  steak, ¾ inch thick

❶ Mix onion, steak sauce, garlic and oregano in bowl. Place steak in nonmetal dish or plastic bag; add steak sauce mixture, turning to coat both sides. Cover; refrigerate for 1 hour, turning occasionally.

❷ Remove steak from marinade; discard marinade. Grill or broil steak for 4 to 6 minutes on each side or until desired doneness.

# Steak with Fennel

MAKES 6 SERVINGS • PREP TIME: 10 MINUTES
MARINATE TIME: 1 HOUR • COOK TIME: 10 MINUTES

⅓ cup A.1. SWEET & TANGY
  Steak Sauce
1 to 2 tablespoons grated orange peel
1 tablespoon white wine vinegar

2 teaspoons crushed fennel seed
2 teaspoons finely chopped garlic
1 (1½-pound) boneless beef top
  sirloin steak, ¾ inch thick

❶ Mix steak sauce, orange peel, vinegar, fennel seed and garlic in bowl. Place steak in nonmetal dish or plastic bag; add steak sauce mixture, turning to coat both sides. Cover; refrigerate for 1 hour, turning occasionally.

❷ Remove steak from marinade; discard marinade. Grill or broil steak for 5 to 7 minutes on each side or until desired doneness.

# Spicy Steak Carbonnade

MAKES 12 SERVINGS • PREP TIME: 20 MINUTES
MARINATE TIME: 1 HOUR • COOK TIME: 12 MINUTES

⅔ cup beer

½ cup chopped onion

⅓ cup A.1. BOLD & SPICY Steak Sauce

½ teaspoon paprika

½ teaspoon chili powder

6 (8-ounce) boneless beef top
   loin steaks, 1 inch thick

❶ Mix beer, onion, steak sauce, paprika and chili powder in small saucepan. Heat to a boil. Reduce heat; simmer for 5 minutes. Cool.

❷ Place steaks in nonmetal dish or plastic bag; add cooled steak sauce mixture, turning to coat both sides. Cover; refrigerate for 1 hour, turning occasionally.

❸ Remove steaks from marinade; place marinade in small saucepan. Heat to a boil. Reduce heat; simmer for 5 minutes. Keep warm.

❹ Grill or broil steaks for 6 to 8 minutes on each side or until desired doneness. Serve with warm carbonnade sauce.

---

### COOKING WITH BEER OR WINE

*When beer or wine boils, much of the alcohol evaporates, leaving just the flavor. However, if you prefer to use a nonalcoholic option, substitute nonalcoholic malted beverage, apple juice or cider for beer and white or regular grape juice for wine.*

# Southern Grilled Steak

⅔ cup A.1. SWEET & TANGY
Steak Sauce
½ cup finely chopped onion

¼ cup bourbon
1 (1½-pound) beef top sirloin steak,
¾ inch thick

❶ Mix steak sauce, onion and bourbon in bowl. Place steak in nonmetal dish
or plastic bag; add steak sauce mixture, turning to coat both sides. Cover;
refrigerate for 1 hour, turning occasionally.

❷ Remove steak from marinade; place marinade in small saucepan; heat to a boil.
Reduce heat; simmer for 5 minutes. Keep warm.

❸ Grill or broil steak for 5 to 7 minutes on each side or until desired doneness.
Serve with warm bourbon sauce.

## MARINATING HINTS

*Meats are marinated either to add flavor or to tenderize.
When marinating for flavor, you can marinate for as little
as 30 minutes in the refrigerator. For tenderizing, you'll
need to allow more time, often several hours or overnight.
It takes that much time for the acid in vinegar, citrus juice
or tomato to tenderize the meat. To be safe, after the
meat is marinated, do not brush the marinade onto
the meat or serve it with the meat, unless you boil it for
at least 2 minutes first.*

# Herbed Mustard Steak

**MAKES 6 SERVINGS • PREP TIME: 15 MINUTES**
**MARINATE TIME: 4 HOURS • COOK TIME: 14 MINUTES**

½ cup A.1. ORIGINAL Steak Sauce
⅓ cup plus 1 tablespoon water, divided
1 (0.7-ounce) envelope Italian salad
    dressing mix

1 tablespoon GREY POUPON
    Dijon Mustard
1 (1½-pound) beef flank steak,
    ¾ inch thick

❶ Mix steak sauce, ⅓ cup water, dressing mix and mustard in bowl. Place steak in nonmetal dish or plastic bag; add steak sauce mixture, turning to coat both sides. Cover; refrigerate for 4 to 24 hours, turning occasionally.

❷ Remove steak from marinade; place marinade and remaining water in small saucepan. Heat to a boil. Reduce heat; simmer for 5 minutes. Keep warm.

❸ Grill or broil steak for 7 to 9 minutes on each side or until desired doneness. Serve with warm mustard sauce.

---

### ADD FLAVOR TO MEAT

*The secret behind a great-tasting steak may be a baste, paste, rub, marinade or sauce. When should each be used?*

**Baste:** *A thin mixture that's brushed onto meat during cooking. It's best for a larger cut that cooks a long time.*

**Paste:** *A thick combination of ingredients that is brushed or spooned onto tender meat as it cooks.*

**Rub:** *A dry mixture that is rubbed onto tender cuts of meat before cooking.*

**Marinade:** *A seasoned liquid that coats meat for a time before cooking to either tenderize or flavor it.*

**Sauce:** *A cooked or stirred mixture that is served with cooked meat.*

HERB-CRUSTED PRIME RIB

# Herb-Crusted Prime Rib

**MAKES 8 TO 10 SERVINGS • PREP TIME: 10 MINUTES**
**COOK TIME: 1¾ HOURS • STAND TIME: 15 MINUTES**

1 (4- to 6-pound) beef rib roast
¼ cup A.1. ORIGINAL Steak Sauce
2 tablespoons fine dry bread crumbs
2 teaspoons snipped fresh rosemary
    *or* ½ teaspoon dried rosemary,
    crumbled

2 teaspoons snipped fresh thyme
    leaves *or* ½ teaspoon dried
    thyme, crumbled

❶ Brush roast with steak sauce. Mix bread crumbs, rosemary and thyme in bowl; sprinkle onto roast, pressing gently into meat.

❷ Place roast, fat side up, on a rack in a shallow roasting pan. Roast at 350°F for 1¾ to 2¾ hours or until internal temperature reaches 140°F for medium rare or 155°F for medium.

❸ After roasting, remove roast from oven; cover with foil. Let stand 15 minutes (internal temperature will rise 5°F during standing).

# Herb Pepper Sirloin Steak

**MAKES 6 SERVINGS • PREP TIME: 10 MINUTES**
**COOK TIME: 10 MINUTES**

¼ cup A.1. ORIGINAL Steak Sauce
2 teaspoons snipped fresh basil *or*
    ½ teaspoon dried basil, crumbled
1½ teaspoons snipped fresh rosemary
    or ½ teaspoon dried rosemary,
    crumbled

½ teaspoon coarse ground black pepper
⅛ teaspoon garlic powder
1 (1½-pound) boneless beef top
    sirloin steak, ¾ inch thick

❶ Mix steak sauce, basil, rosemary, pepper and garlic powder in bowl; brush onto both sides of steak.

❷ Grill or broil steak for 5 to 7 minutes on each side or until desired doneness.

# Cajun-Style Steaks

**MAKES 8 SERVINGS • PREP TIME: 5 MINUTES**
**COOK TIME: 8 MINUTES**

¼ cup A.1. BOLD & SPICY *or*
    A.1. ORIGINAL Steak Sauce
¾ teaspoon *each* garlic powder, onion
    powder and ground black pepper

½ teaspoon ground white pepper
¼ teaspoon ground red pepper
4 (8-ounce) boneless beef top loin
    steaks, ¾ inch thick

❶ Mix steak sauce, garlic powder, onion powder and peppers in bowl; brush onto both sides of steaks.

❷ Grill or broil steaks for 4 to 6 minutes on each side or until desired doneness.

# Grilled Southwest Steak

**MAKES 6 SERVINGS • PREP TIME: 20 MINUTES**
**MARINATE TIME: 6 HOURS • COOK TIME: 14 MINUTES**

½ cup A.1. BOLD & SPICY Steak Sauce

2 tablespoons vegetable oil

3 jalapeño peppers, seeded and chopped

⅓ cup finely chopped onion

2 cloves garlic, finely chopped

2 tablespoons snipped fresh cilantro

1 (1½-pound) beef flank steak,
     ¾ inch thick

❶ Mix steak sauce, oil, peppers, onion, garlic and cilantro in bowl. Place steak in nonmetal dish or plastic bag; add steak sauce mixture, turning to coat both sides. Cover; refrigerate for 6 hours or overnight, turning steak occasionally.

❷ Remove steak from marinade; place marinade in small saucepan. Heat to a boil. Reduce heat; simmer 5 minutes. Cover; keep warm.

❸ Grill or broil steak for 7 to 9 minutes on each side or until desired doneness, brushing often with marinade.

# Lemon Pepper Steaks

**MAKES 4 SERVINGS • PREP TIME: 5 MINUTES**
**COOK TIME: 8 MINUTES**

¼ cup A.1. ORIGINAL Steak Sauce

1½ teaspoons grated lemon peel

1 clove garlic, finely chopped

½ teaspoon coarse ground black pepper

2 (8-ounce) boneless beef top loin
     steaks, ¾ inch thick

❶ Mix steak sauce, lemon peel, garlic and pepper in bowl; brush onto both sides of steaks.

❷ Grill or broil steaks for 4 to 6 minutes on each side or until desired doneness.

**NOTE:** For the best lemon flavor, grate or finely shred just the zest (the yellow outer coating) of a lemon.

SAVORY GRILLED TOURNEDOS

# Savory Grilled Tournedos

**MAKES 8 SERVINGS • PREP TIME: 15 MINUTES
COOK TIME: 12 MINUTES**

8 slices bacon (about 5 ounces)
8 (4-ounce) beef tenderloin steaks,
    1 inch thick
⅓ cup A.1. BOLD & SPICY *or*
    A.1. ORIGINAL Steak Sauce

¼ cup ketchup
¼ cup orange marmalade
2 tablespoons lemon juice
2 tablespoons finely chopped onion
1 clove garlic, finely chopped

❶ Wrap a bacon slice around edge of each steak; secure with string or toothpick.

❷ Mix steak sauce, ketchup, marmalade, lemon juice, onion and garlic; reserve ⅔ cup steak sauce mixture.

❸ Grill or broil steaks for 6 to 8 minutes on each side or until desired doneness, brushing often with the remaining sauce mixture. Serve steaks with reserved steak sauce mixture.

# British Isles T-Bone Steaks

MAKES 4 SERVINGS • PREP TIME: 5 MINUTES
COOK TIME: 14 MINUTES

⅓ cup A.1. ORIGINAL Steak Sauce

2 tablespoons malt *or* cider vinegar

2 teaspoons dry mustard

2 (1-pound) beef loin T-bone steaks, 1 inch thick

❶ Mix steak sauce, vinegar and mustard in bowl.

❷ Grill or broil steaks for 7 to 9 minutes on each side or until desired doneness, brushing with steak sauce mixture occasionally.

# Bloody Mary Steaks

MAKES 8 SERVINGS • PREP TIME: 5 MINUTES
COOK TIME: 8 MINUTES

⅓ cup A.1. BOLD & SPICY Steak Sauce

2 tablespoons tomato paste

2 tablespoons prepared horseradish

1 tablespoon grated lemon peel

1 teaspoon celery seed

4 (8-ounce) beef top loin steaks, ¾ inch thick

❶ Mix steak sauce, tomato paste, horseradish, lemon peel and celery seed in bowl.

❷ Grill or broil steaks for 4 to 6 minutes on each side or until desired doneness, brushing with steak sauce mixture occasionally.

# Oriental Peanut-Ginger Steaks

**MAKES 8 SERVINGS • PREP TIME: 10 MINUTES**
**COOK TIME: 8 MINUTES**

½ cup A.1. SWEET & TANGY
Steak Sauce

3 tablespoons creamy peanut butter

2 tablespoons soy sauce

1 tablespoon grated fresh ginger

Grated peel and juice of 1 lime

4 (8-ounce) boneless beef top loin
steaks, ¾ inch thick

❶ Mix steak sauce, peanut butter, soy sauce, ginger and lime peel and juice.
Reserve ½ cup steak sauce mixture.

❷ Grill or broil steaks for 4 to 6 minutes on each side or until desired doneness,
brushing occasionally with remaining sauce mixture. Serve with reserved steak
sauce mixture.

# Horseradish-Cumin Steaks

**MAKES 8 SERVINGS • PREP TIME: 5 MINUTES**
**COOK TIME: 6 MINUTES**

⅓ cup A.1. ORIGINAL Steak Sauce

2 tablespoons prepared horseradish

1 teaspoon finely chopped garlic

2 teaspoons ground cumin

4 (8-ounce) boneless beef rib-eye
steaks, ¾ inch thick

❶ Mix steak sauce, horseradish, garlic and cumin.

❷ Grill or broil steaks for 3 to 5 minutes on each side or until desired doneness,
brushing frequently with steak sauce mixture.

# Short Ribs with Sweet-and-Spicy Molasses Sauce

**MAKES 6 SERVINGS • PREP TIME: 15 MINUTES**
**COOK TIME: 1³/₄ HOURS**

3 to 4 pounds beef short ribs,
    cut into serving-size pieces
4 cups water
1 large onion, sliced and separated
    into rings
Celery leaves

¹/₃ cup A.1. BOLD & SPICY
    Steak Sauce
3 tablespoons molasses
1 tablespoon snipped fresh thyme
    leaves *or* 1 teaspoon dried
    thyme, crumbled

❶ Place ribs in heavy large pot; add water, onion and celery leaves. Heat to a boil. Reduce heat; cover and simmer for 1¹/₂ to 2 hours or until tender.

❷ Remove ribs from pot. Skim fat from cooking liquid. Strain and reserve ¹/₄ cup cooking liquid.

❸ Mix reserved cooking liquid, steak sauce, molasses and thyme in bowl. Reserve ¹/₃ cup steak sauce mixture.

❹ Grill or broil ribs for 15 minutes, turning and brushing with remaining steak sauce mixture every 5 minutes.

❺ Heat reserved steak sauce mixture to a boil. Serve with ribs.

**NOTE:** To get a jump start on dinner, simmer the ribs, skim the fat and strain the cooking liquid the night before. Cover and refrigerate until it's time to light the coals.

## STICK TO RIBS

*For some people, ribs are the essence of barbecue. Since beef ribs require long, slow cooking, they need to simmer in water awhile to become tender. If you don't want to mess with bones, purchase boneless beef ribs instead.*

# Tex-Mex Beef Ribs

**MAKES 6 SERVINGS • PREP TIME: 10 MINUTES**
**COOK TIME: 1¾ HOURS**

3 to 4 pounds beef short ribs, cut into
    serving-size pieces
1 cup A.1. SWEET & TANGY
    Steak Sauce

⅓ cup picante sauce
1 teaspoon chili powder
½ teaspoon dry mustard

❶ Place ribs in heavy large pot; add water to cover. Heat to a boil. Reduce heat; cover and simmer for 1½ to 2 hours or until tender. Drain ribs.

❷ Mix steak sauce, picante sauce, chili powder and mustard in small saucepan; heat to a boil. Reduce heat; simmer, uncovered, for 5 minutes, stirring once.

❸ Grill or broil ribs for 15 minutes, turning and brushing with ½ cup steak sauce mixture every 5 minutes. Serve ribs with remaining steak sauce mixture.

# Tangy Barbecued Beef Ribs

**MAKES 6 SERVINGS • PREP TIME: 10 MINUTES**
**COOK TIME: 70 MINUTES**

3 to 4 pounds beef back ribs, cut into
    individual ribs and halved
½ cup A.1. SWEET & TANGY
    Steak Sauce

¼ cup finely chopped onion
1 clove garlic, finely chopped
½ to ¾ teaspoon TABASCO®
    Pepper Sauce

❶ Place ribs in heavy large pot; add water to cover. Heat to a boil. Reduce heat; cover and simmer for 1 hour or until tender. Drain ribs.

❷ Mix steak sauce, onion, garlic and pepper sauce in bowl; set aside.

❸ Grill or broil ribs for 10 to 12 minutes or until glazed, turning and brushing with steak sauce mixture.

# Teriyaki Steak Skewers

**MAKES 4 SERVINGS • PREP TIME: 20 MINUTES**
**MARINATE TIME: 1 HOUR • COOK TIME: 4 MINUTES**

½ cup A.1. ORIGINAL Steak Sauce

2 tablespoons packed brown sugar

2 tablespoons soy sauce

2 cloves garlic, finely chopped

1 teaspoon ground ginger

1 (1-pound) boneless beef sirloin
  steak, 1 inch thick

2 medium red *and/or* green bell
  peppers, cut into squares

2 cups fresh *or* canned
  pineapple chunks

Hot cooked spaghetti, optional

❶ Mix steak sauce, brown sugar, soy sauce, garlic and ginger in bowl. Thinly slice steak; place in nonmetal bowl or plastic bag. Add ¼ cup steak sauce mixture; stir to coat steak strips. Cover; refrigerate at least 1 hour, stirring occasionally.

❷ Remove meat from marinade; discard marinade. Alternately thread steak, peppers and pineapple onto 8 (12-inch) skewers.

❸ Grill or broil kabobs for 4 to 6 minutes or until desired doneness, turning once and brushing occasionally with remaining steak sauce mixture. Serve with hot cooked pasta, if desired.

**TERIYAKI STEAK SKEWERS**

# Surf-and-Turf Kabobs

**MAKES 4 SERVINGS • PREP TIME: 30 MINUTES**
**COOK TIME: 6 MINUTES**

¼ cup A.1. SWEET & TANGY
    Steak Sauce

1 tablespoon grated lemon peel

2 teaspoons ground paprika

¼ teaspoon ground black pepper

1 (8-ounce) boneless beef top
    sirloin steak

½ pound large shrimp (about 20),
    shelled and deveined

1 large red bell pepper, cut
    into squares

3 green onions, cut into 2-inch pieces

❶ Mix steak sauce, lemon peel, paprika and ground black pepper in bowl; set aside. Thinly slice steak.

❷ Alternately thread steak, shrimp, red pepper and green onions onto 8 (12-inch) skewers.

❸ Grill or broil kabobs for 6 to 10 minutes or until shrimp turn pink and meat is done, turning once and brushing occasionally with steak sauce mixture.

# Herbed Tomato Beef Kabobs

**MAKES 4 SERVINGS • PREP TIME: 20 MINUTES**
**COOK TIME: 8 MINUTES**

½ cup A.1. ORIGINAL Steak Sauce

1 (0.7-ounce) envelope Italian salad
    dressing mix

2 tablespoons water

1 (1-pound) boneless beef top sirloin
    steak, cut into 1-inch cubes

1 medium green *or* red bell pepper,
    cut into squares

16 small mushroom caps

8 cherry tomatoes

❶ Combine steak sauce, salad dressing mix and water in small saucepan. Heat to a boil. Set aside. Alternately thread beef, pepper and mushroom caps onto 8 (12-inch) skewers.

❷ Grill or broil kabobs for 8 to 12 minutes or until desired doneness, turning and brushing occasionally with steak sauce mixture. Add cherry tomatoes to skewers the last 1 to 2 minutes of cooking.

# Beef-and-Bacon Shish Kabobs

**MAKES 4 SERVINGS • PREP TIME: 25 MINUTES**
**MARINATE TIME: 1 HOUR • COOK TIME: 8 MINUTES**

½ cup A.1. SWEET & TANGY
    Steak Sauce
¼ cup dry sherry
2 tablespoons honey
1 (1-pound) boneless beef top
    sirloin steak, cut into
    1-inch cubes

20 slices bacon, halved crosswise
    (about 1 pound)
1 large onion, cut into wedges
1 large green *or* red bell pepper,
    cut into squares
16 small mushroom caps

❶ Mix steak sauce, sherry and honey in bowl. Place steak cubes in nonmetal dish or plastic bag; add ¼ cup steak sauce mixture, stirring to coat cubes. Cover; refrigerate for 1 hour, stirring occasionally.

❷ Cook bacon in 12-inch skillet until done but not crisp. Drain on paper towels. Cool slightly.

❸ Remove beef cubes from marinade; discard marinade. Wrap half bacon slice around each cube. Alternately thread wrapped beef cubes, onion, pepper and mushrooms onto 8 (12-inch) skewers.

❹ Grill or broil for 8 to 12 minutes or until desired doneness, turning and brushing occasionally with remaining steak sauce mixture.

## CUTTING BEEF INTO STRIPS

*Cutting thin strips of meat can be a challenge, but there's a nifty way to do it. Simply put the steak in the freezer until it gets slightly firm (not frozen solid), then thinly slice across the grain.*

**HEARTY AMERICAN CHEESEBURGER AND OVEN FRIES (RECIPE, PAGE 80)**

# Hearty American Cheeseburgers

**MAKES 4 SERVINGS • PREP TIME: 15 MINUTES**
**COOK TIME: 10 MINUTES**

1½ pounds lean ground beef

¾ cup A.1. THICK & HEARTY Steak
   Sauce, divided

⅓ cup chopped dill pickle

1 large yellow *or* red onion, cut into
   ¼-inch-thick slices

4 slices American cheese

4 onion rolls, split

4 lettuce leaves

4 slices tomato

❶ Shape beef into 4 (½-inch-thick) patties; set aside. Mix ½ cup steak sauce and dill pickle in bowl; set aside.

❷ Grill or broil onion slices about 5 minutes on each side or until tender, brushing with 2 tablespoons steak sauce.

❸ Grill or broil burgers for 5 to 7 minutes on each side or until no pink remains, brushing with remaining steak sauce. Top with cheese.

❹ Top roll bottoms with lettuce leaves, burgers, onion slices, tomato and steak sauce mixture; replace roll tops.

# Horseradish Burgers

MAKES 4 SERVINGS • PREP TIME: 10 MINUTES
COOK TIME: 12 MINUTES

1½ pounds lean ground beef

½ cup A.1. THICK & HEARTY Steak
  Sauce, divided

2 tablespoons prepared horseradish

2 tablespoons finely chopped parsley

2 tablespoons finely chopped
  green onion

4 thick slices Muenster *or*
  Swiss cheese

4 rye rolls, split and toasted

❶ Shape beef into 4 (¾-inch-thick) patties; set aside. Mix 6 tablespoons steak sauce, horseradish, parsley and green onion in bowl; set aside.

❷ Grill or broil burgers for 6 to 8 minutes on each side or until no pink remains, brushing with remaining steak sauce. Top with cheese.

❸ Top roll bottoms with burgers and horseradish sauce; replace roll tops.

# Bacon Blue Cheese Burgers

MAKES 4 SERVINGS • PREP TIME: 10 MINUTES
COOK TIME: 10 MINUTES

1 pound lean ground beef

½ cup A.1. THICK & HEARTY Steak
  Sauce, divided

½ cup crumbled blue cheese
  (2 ounces)

4 sandwich rolls, split

4 lettuce leaves

4 slices red onion

4 slices bacon, cooked and halved
  (about 3 ounces)

❶ Mix ground beef and 3 tablespoons steak sauce in bowl. Shape mixture into 4 (½-inch-thick) patties; set aside. Mix remaining steak sauce and blue cheese in bowl; set aside.

❷ Grill or broil burgers for 5 to 7 minutes on each side or until no pink remains.

❸ Spread roll bottoms and roll tops with steak sauce mixture. Top roll bottoms with lettuce leaves, onion slices, burgers and bacon. Replace roll tops.

# Sonoma Burgers

MAKES 4 SERVINGS • PREP TIME: 10 MINUTES
COOK TIME: 12 MINUTES

1½ pounds lean ground beef
½ cup A.1. THICK & HEARTY
 Steak Sauce, divided
3 tablespoons snipped fresh basil
2 tablespoons chopped oil-packed
 sun-dried tomatoes

1 tablespoon toasted pine nuts *or*
 PLANTERS Walnuts, chopped
4 sourdough rolls *or* 4-inch
 squares focaccia bread,
 split and toasted
2 ounces goat cheese *or* shredded
 farmer's cheese (optional)

❶ Shape beef into 4 (¾-inch-thick) patties, shaping into squares if using focaccia bread; set aside. Mix 6 tablespoons steak sauce, basil, tomatoes and nuts in bowl; set aside.

❷ Grill or broil burgers for 6 to 8 minutes on each side or until no pink remains, brushing with remaining steak sauce.

❸ Spread roll tops with cheese, if desired. Top roll bottoms with burgers and steak sauce mixture; replace roll tops.

### SHAPE AND FREEZE PATTIES AHEAD

*You can save money by purchasing ground beef in large quantities and freezing some. To speed thawing and preparation before mealtime, form ground beef into patties immediately after purchasing. Top each patty with plastic wrap or foil, stack, seal in airtight freezer containers and freeze up to 4 months. When you need them, simply remove the desired number of patties and reseal the rest.*

# SALADS

There's nothing like

a crisp, green salad to

complement meat. The two

have paired up on menus

almost since the first steak

house opened its doors.

But today the salad options

are more diverse and

vibrant than ever.

**CAESAR SALAD**
(RECIPE, PAGE 64)

# Caesar Salad

*Recipe is pictured on pages 62 and 63.*

½ cup olive oil

3 anchovy fillets, optional

2 tablespoons lemon juice

1 teaspoon Worcestershire sauce

1 clove garlic, halved

10 cups torn romaine leaves

1 cup prepared garlic-flavored croutons

¼ cup shredded Parmesan cheese

Coarse ground black pepper, to taste

❶ Mix oil, anchovy fillets (if desired), lemon juice, Worcestershire sauce and garlic in blender container. Blend until smooth. Cover; refrigerate until serving time.

❷ Mix romaine, croutons and Parmesan cheese in large bowl. Stir dressing and pour over salad; toss to coat. Season with pepper to taste. Serve immediately.

# Mixed Green Salad with Artichokes

1 (6- or 6½-ounce) jar marinated
  artichoke hearts

3 tablespoons mayonnaise *or*
  salad dressing

6 cups torn mixed salad greens

16 red *and/or* yellow cherry
  tomatoes, halved

Toasted sesame seeds, optional

❶ Drain artichokes, reserving 2 tablespoons of liquid. Cut up any large pieces of artichokes into bite-size pieces. Stir reserved artichoke liquid into mayonnaise or salad dressing.

❷ Mix greens, artichokes and cherry tomatoes in large bowl; toss with mayonnaise mixture. Sprinkle with sesame seeds, if desired.

**MIXED GREEN SALAD WITH ARTICHOKES**

# Greens with Dijon Dressing

MAKES 4 SERVINGS • PREP TIME: 15 MINUTES

4 cups torn mixed salad greens

1 (8-ounce) package fresh mushrooms, sliced (about 3 cups)

1 medium red *and/or* yellow tomato, cut into thin wedges

3 tablespoons vinegar

2 tablespoons vegetable oil

1 tablespoon GREY POUPON Country Dijon Mustard

1 tablespoon honey

❶ Mix greens, mushrooms and tomato in large bowl; set aside.

❷ Mix vinegar, oil, mustard and honey in bowl. Pour over greens mixture. Toss to coat.

**NOTE:** Make the dressing ahead of time—its flavor will improve as it stands in the refrigerator. Be sure to stir the dressing before using it.

# Romaine and Walnut Salad

MAKES 4 SERVINGS • PREP TIME: 15 MINUTES

4 cups torn romaine leaves

2 plum tomatoes, sliced

½ cup sliced fresh mushrooms

¼ cup PLANTERS Walnuts, chopped

¼ cup red wine vinegar

2 tablespoons vegetable oil

2 tablespoons honey

¼ teaspoon dry mustard

❶ Mix romaine, tomatoes, mushrooms and walnuts in large bowl; set aside.

❷ Mix vinegar, oil, honey and dry mustard in bowl. Pour over romaine mixture. Toss to coat.

**NOTE:** For extra flavor, toast the walnuts in a skillet or oven before adding them to the salad.

# Wilted Spinach Salad

**MAKES 4 SERVINGS • PREP TIME: 15 MINUTES**

1 cup sliced fresh mushrooms

⅓ cup sliced green onions

⅓ cup clear Italian salad dressing

2 teaspoons honey

6 cups torn spinach leaves

2 tablespoons cooked bacon pieces

❶ Mix mushrooms, green onions, salad dressing and honey in 12-inch skillet. Heat to a boil; boil for 1 minute.

❷ Add spinach; toss for 15 to 30 seconds or until spinach just begins to wilt. Transfer to large bowl; sprinkle with bacon. Serve immediately.

## CLEANING GREENS

*Before using fresh spinach or other leafy fresh greens, remove any tough stems or cores, wash the leaves in cold water (you may need to rinse spinach leaves several times to get rid of any sand), and pat the leaves dry with paper towels. For head lettuce, hit the stem end sharply on a countertop, twist the core and lift it out. Then, wash the lettuce core side up under cold running water and invert the head to let the water run out. To store the cleaned greens, place them in a plastic bag or airtight container and refrigerate for up to 5 days.*

# Tomatoes with Basil Vinaigrette
### MAKES 4 SERVINGS • PREP TIME: 15 MINUTES

Lettuce leaves
2 medium tomatoes, cored and
thinly sliced
3 ounces Mozzarella cheese, sliced
2 tablespoons olive oil
1 tablespoon snipped fresh basil

1 tablespoon balsamic vinegar *or*
2 teaspoons cider vinegar
1 small clove garlic, finely chopped
1/8 teaspoon salt
Coarse ground black pepper

❶ Line serving platter with lettuce leaves. Arrange tomatoes and cheese on platter.

❷ Mix oil, basil, vinegar, garlic and salt in bowl. Drizzle oil mixture over tomato and cheese slices. Refrigerate until serving.

❸ Sprinkle with pepper before serving.

# Asparagus and Tomato Salad
### MAKES 4 SERVINGS • PREP TIME: 25 MINUTES

1/4 cup mayonnaise or salad dressing
1 tablespoon GREY POUPON
Dijon Mustard
1 teaspoon vinegar
Boston *or* Bibb lettuce leaves

12 ounces asparagus spears, cleaned
and cooked
2 hard-cooked eggs, sliced
2 red *or* yellow plum tomatoes, cut into
wedges, or 6 to 8 red *or* yellow
baby pear tomatoes, halved

❶ Mix mayonnaise or salad dressing, mustard and vinegar in bowl.

❷ Line 4 salad plates with lettuce. Arrange asparagus, egg slices and tomatoes on plates; drizzle with mayonnaise mixture.

**TOMATOES WITH BASIL VINAIGRETTE**

# Asparagus and Wilted Greens

**MAKES 4 SERVINGS • PREP TIME: 25 MINUTES**

12 ounces asparagus, cleaned and cut into 2-inch pieces (about 2 cups)

4 slices bacon

1 small onion, sliced and separated into rings

2 tablespoons tarragon-flavored white wine vinegar *or* 2 tablespoons white wine vinegar and ¼ teaspoon dried tarragon, crumbled

1 tablespoon sugar

⅛ teaspoon salt

3 cups torn Boston *or* Bibb lettuce

❶ Heat a small amount of water to a boil in medium saucepan. Add asparagus; cover and cook for 4 to 6 minutes or until tender-crisp. Drain.

❷ Cook bacon in large skillet over medium heat until crisp. Remove bacon, reserving drippings in skillet. Drain bacon on paper towels. Crumble bacon; set aside.

❸ Cook and stir onion in drippings in skillet over medium heat about 5 minutes or until tender. Stir in vinegar, sugar and salt. Heat to a boil. Add asparagus, bacon and lettuce. Toss 30 seconds or until lettuce just begins to wilt. Transfer to large bowl. Serve immediately.

## WILTING GREENS FOR SALADS

*A wilted salad's success comes from the unexpected sensation of warmth on cool greens. Timing is everything, for once the hot dressing hits the greens, it begins to "cook" them. Toss the salad just before serving so you won't be stuck with soggy lettuce.*

# Wilted Spinach with Apples and Feta Cheese

**MAKES 4 SERVINGS • PREP TIME: 20 MINUTES**

6 cups torn spinach leaves
¼ cup sliced green onions
3 slices bacon
3 tablespoons vinegar

1 teaspoon sugar
1 cup sliced *or* chopped apple
⅓ cup crumbled feta cheese

❶ Mix spinach and green onions in large bowl. Set aside.

❷ Cook bacon in large skillet over medium heat until crisp. Remove bacon, reserving 2 tablespoons drippings in skillet. Drain bacon on paper towels. Crumble bacon; set aside.

❸ Stir vinegar and sugar into reserved drippings; heat to a boil. Add spinach mixture to skillet. Toss 30 to 60 seconds or until spinach just begins to wilt. Remove from heat. Add apple and cheese. Toss gently to mix. Transfer to large bowl. Sprinkle with crumbled bacon. Serve immediately.

# Raspberry Gorgonzola Salad

**MAKES 4 SERVINGS • PREP TIME: 20 MINUTES**

4 cups torn Boston *or* Bibb lettuce leaves
1½ cups shredded red cabbage
1 small red bell pepper, cut into thin
   strips (about ¾ cup)
1 medium red *or* Bartlett pear,
   cored and sliced (about 1 cup)

⅓ cup crumbled Gorgonzola *or*
   blue cheese
⅓ cup bottled raspberry *or*
   balsamic vinaigrette

❶ Mix lettuce and cabbage in large bowl; divide evenly among 4 salad plates. Top with pepper, pear and cheese.

❷ Drizzle with vinaigrette.

# SIDE DISHES

A steak deserves first-rate

partners on the plate—and

have we got 'em! From garden

vegetables in savory sauces

to potatoes—mashed, baked

or roasted—look no further

for the perfect match (or two).

The good news: they're easy

to prepare as well.

CREAMED SPINACH
(RECIPE, PAGE 74)
OVEN FRIES
(RECIPE, PAGE 80)

## Green Beans Amandine

MAKES 2 TO 3 SERVINGS • PREP TIME: 10 MINUTES
COOK TIME: 25 MINUTES

8 ounces fresh green beans *or* one
9-ounce package frozen cut
*or* French-cut green beans
1 tablespoon margarine *or* butter

2 tablespoons PLANTERS Sliced
Almonds
1 teaspoon lemon juice

❶ Cut fresh beans into 2-inch pieces. Heat a small amount of water to a boil in saucepan. Add fresh beans; cover and cook about 20 minutes or until tender-crisp. (Or, cook frozen beans according to package directions.) Drain beans; keep warm.

❷ Heat margarine or butter in small skillet over medium heat until melted. Add almonds; cook until golden. Remove from heat; stir in lemon juice. Stir almond mixture into beans.

## Creamed Spinach

MAKES 2 TO 3 SERVINGS • PREP TIME: 5 MINUTES
COOK TIME: 12 MINUTES

*Recipe is pictured on pages 72 and 73.*

2 tablespoons water
10 ounces chopped spinach
½ cup soft cream cheese

1 to 2 tablespoons milk
¼ teaspoon seasoned salt
2 tablespoons cooked bacon pieces

❶ Heat water to a boil in medium saucepan. Add spinach; cover and cook for 2 to 3 minutes or until wilted. Drain well; set aside.

❷ Add cream cheese, milk and salt to same saucepan; cook and stir over low heat until smooth. Stir in cooked spinach; heat through. Transfer to large bowl. Sprinkle with bacon.

**NOTE:** To substitute frozen spinach for fresh spinach, use 1 (10-ounce) package frozen leaf spinach and cook it according to package directions. Continue as above.

**GREEN BEANS AMANDINE**

# Asparagus Dijon

**MAKES 6 SERVINGS • PREP TIME: 10 MINUTES**
**COOK TIME: 4 MINUTES**

asparagus spears,
or two 10-ounce
frozen asparagus spears
cream
e *or* salad dressing

2 tablespoons sliced green onion
1 tablespoon GREY POUPON
Dijon Mustard
¾ teaspoon grated lemon peel
Milk, optional

❶ Heat a small amount of water to a boil in large saucepan. Add asparagus; cover and cook for 4 to 8 minutes or until tender-crisp. (Or, cook frozen asparagus according to package directions.) Drain; keep warm.

❷ Mix sour cream, mayonnaise or salad dressing, green onion, mustard and lemon peel. Thin sauce with a little milk, if desired. To serve, spoon sauce over asparagus.

#  Onion Rings

**MAKES 6 SERVINGS • PREP TIME: 15 MINUTES**
**COOK TIME: 16 MINUTES**

¾ cup all-purpose flour
⅔ cup milk
1 egg
1 tablespoon vegetable oil
¼ teaspoon salt

Vegetable oil *or* shortening
for deep-fat frying
4 medium mild yellow *or* white
onions, sliced ¼ inch thick
and separated into rings

❶ Mix flour, milk, egg, 1 tablespoon oil and salt in medium bowl. Beat with rotary beater just until smooth.

❷ Heat 1 inch oil or shortening in large skillet to 365°F. Using a fork, dip onion rings into batter; drain off excess batter. Fry onion rings, a few at a time, in a single layer in skillet for 2 to 3 minutes or until golden, stirring once or twice with a fork to separate rings. Remove rings from oil; drain on paper towels.

# Easy Risotto

MAKES 4 SERVINGS • PREP TIME: 5 MINUTES
COOK TIME: 30 MINUTES • STAND TIME: 5 MINUTES

½ cup chopped onion

1 tablespoon margarine *or* butter

⅔ cup Arborio *or* long-grain rice

2 cups water

½ teaspoon instant beef bouillon granules

⅛ teaspoon ground black pepper

¼ cup grated Parmesan *or* Romano cheese

❶ Cook and stir onion in margarine or butter in medium saucepan over medium heat about 5 minutes or until tender. Add uncooked rice. Cook and stir for 2 minutes. Carefully stir in water, bouillon granules and pepper; heat to a boil. Reduce heat; cover and simmer for 20 minutes (do not lift cover).

❷ Remove from heat. Let stand, covered, for 5 minutes. Rice should be tender but slightly firm, and the mixture should be creamy. (If necessary, stir in a little water to reach desired consistency.) Stir in cheese.

## RISOTTO AND ITALIAN RICE

*Risotto (rih ZOT oh) is a northern Italian rice dish. Italian cooks make it with Arborio rice, which you'll find in gourmet shops or Italian specialty food stores. Arborio is best for producing the traditional creamy consistency, but you can substitute a long- or medium-grain rice. The texture of the finished risotto should be creamy, but not sticky or runny. The rice itself should be tender, but still slightly firm.*

# Herb-Roasted Potatoes

MAKES 6 SERVINGS • PREP TIME: 10 MINUTES
COOK TIME: 35 MINUTES

⅓ cup GREY POUPON
Dijon Mustard
2 tablespoons olive oil
1 clove garlic, finely chopped

½ teaspoon dried Italian seasoning
6 medium red-skinned potatoes
(2 pounds), cleaned and
cut into chunks

❶ Mix all ingredients except potatoes in small bowl.

❷ Place potatoes in greased 13x9x2-inch baking pan; pour mustard mixture over and toss.

❸ Bake at 425°F for 35 to 40 minutes or until potatoes are fork tender, stirring occasionally.

# Herb-Buttered Mushrooms

MAKES 4 SERVINGS • PREP TIME: 10 MINUTES
COOK TIME: 7 MINUTES

*Recipe is pictured on page 39 and on front cover.*

1 pound medium fresh mushrooms,
cleaned and halved
2 tablespoons chopped shallots
3 cloves garlic, finely chopped
2 tablespoons margarine *or* butter

2 tablespoons dry sherry
1 teaspoon dried Italian seasoning
¼ teaspoon salt
⅛ to ¼ teaspoon coarse ground
black pepper

❶ Cook and stir mushrooms, shallots and garlic in margarine or butter in large skillet over medium-high heat until tender.

❷ Stir in sherry, Italian seasoning, salt and pepper. Heat through.

**HERB-ROASTED POTATOES**

# Oven Fries

MAKES 4 SERVINGS • PREP TIME: 10 MINUTES
COOK TIME: 25 MINUTES

*Recipe is pictured on pages 58, 72 and 73.*

| | |
|---|---|
| 3 medium russet potatoes (about 1 pound), cleaned | 1 teaspoon paprika |
| 2 tablespoons margarine *or* butter, melted | ¾ teaspoon garlic salt |
| | ½ teaspoon dried thyme, crumbled |
| | ⅛ teaspoon ground red pepper |

❶ Cut potatoes lengthwise into 8 wedges. Arrange wedges in single layer, skin side down, on 15½x10½x1-inch baking pan.

❷ Mix margarine or butter, paprika, garlic salt, thyme and pepper in bowl; brush onto wedges.

❸ Bake at 450°F for 25 minutes or until golden, stirring occasionally.

# Garlic Mashed Potatoes

MAKES 6 SERVINGS • PREP TIME: 15 MINUTES
COOK TIME: 20 MINUTES

| | |
|---|---|
| 6 medium potatoes (about 2 pounds), cleaned, peeled and cubed | 4 cloves garlic, finely chopped |
| 1 medium onion, chopped (about ½ cup) | ¼ cup margarine *or* butter, melted |
| | ¼ to ½ cup milk |
| | Salt and ground black pepper, to taste |

❶ Heat a large amount of salted water to a boil in large saucepan. Add potatoes, onion and garlic; cover and cook about 20 minutes or until potatoes are tender. Drain.

❷ Beat potato mixture in large bowl with mixer at medium speed. Gradually beat in margarine or butter and milk at low speed until smooth. Stir in salt and pepper to taste.

# Cheesy Twice-Baked Potatoes

**MAKES 4 SERVINGS • PREP TIME: 15 MINUTES**
**MICROWAVE TIME: 12 MINUTES • COOK TIME: 20 MINUTES**

*Recipe is pictured on page 17.*

4 medium russet potatoes (about
    1¼ pounds), cleaned and baked
½ cup shredded cheddar cheese
    (2 ounces)

½ cup cream cheese with chives
    and onion
⅛ teaspoon ground black pepper
1 to 2 tablespoons milk, optional
2 tablespoons snipped fresh chives

❶ Cut a lengthwise slice from the top of each potato; discard skin from slice and place pulp in bowl. Gently scoop out the inside of each potato, leaving a ¼-inch-thick shell. Add potato pulp to bowl.

❷ Mash potato pulp with potato masher or beat with electric mixer at low speed. Beat in cheese, cream cheese and pepper until smooth. Stir in milk to desired consistency. Stir in chives. Pipe or spoon potato mixture into potato shells. Place shells in 2-quart-square baking dish.

❸ Bake at 425°F for 20 to 25 minutes or until heated through and light brown.

**NOTE:** You can use chopped green onion instead of chives.

# Roasted Thyme Potato Slices

**MAKES 4 SERVINGS • PREP TIME: 10 MINUTES**
**COOK TIME: 40 MINUTES**

4 medium russet potatoes (about
    1¼ pounds), cleaned
¼ cup margarine *or* butter, melted

1 to 1¼ teaspoons TABASCO®
    Pepper Sauce
½ to ¾ teaspoon dried thyme, crumbled
½ teaspoon salt

❶ Cut potatoes into ¼-inch-thick slices. Place slices in greased 13x9x2-inch baking pan. Mix margarine or butter, pepper sauce, thyme and salt. Drizzle over potatoes; toss to coat.

❷ Bake at 425°F for 40 to 45 minutes or until potatoes are tender and light brown, stirring occasionally.

# DESSERTS

*Save room for the dessert cart.*

*Lick your lips over all-time*

*champs like cheesecake,*

*apple pie, bread pudding*

*and the ultimate in chocolate*

*creations. Each has a twist*

*to ensure it's as easy*

*to fix as it is to enjoy.*

HAZELNUT CHOCOLATE DECADENCE
(RECIPE, PAGE 84)

# Hazelnut Chocolate Decadence

**MAKES 16 SERVINGS • PREP TIME: 45 MINUTES**
**COOK TIME: 40 MINUTES • COOL TIME: 3 HOURS**
**STAND TIME: 30 MINUTES**

*Recipe is pictured on pages 82 and 83.*

1¾ cups hazelnuts

   3 tablespoons margarine *or* butter, melted

   2 (8-ounce) packages semisweet chocolate, chopped

1½ cups heavy cream, divided

   6 eggs

   1 teaspoon vanilla

   ⅓ cup all-purpose flour

   ⅓ cup sugar

❶ Finely chop hazelnuts; mix with margarine or butter in bowl. Press onto bottom and 1½ inches up side of a 9-inch springform pan; set aside.

❷ Heat and stir chocolate and 1 cup cream in heavy medium saucepan over low heat just until chocolate melts. Remove from heat. Cool to room temperature.

❸ Beat eggs and vanilla in large bowl with electric mixer at low speed until combined. Blend in flour and sugar. Beat at high speed about 10 minutes or until slightly thickened. Fold about one-fourth of the egg mixture into chocolate mixture. Fold chocolate mixture into remaining egg mixture. Spread batter into prepared crust.

❹ Bake in preheated 325°F oven for 40 to 45 minutes or until slightly puffed around outer edge (center will be slightly soft). Cool at room temperature for 3 to 4 hours. Cover and refrigerate.

❺ Remove side of pan. Let stand at room temperature for 30 minutes before serving. Beat remaining cream in small bowl with mixer at medium speed just until stiff peaks form. Garnish with whipped cream.

# Fudge Brownie Pie

**MAKES 8 SERVINGS • PREP TIME: 15 MINUTES**
**COOK TIME: 30 MINUTES • COOL TIME: 30 MINUTES**

½ cup margarine *or* butter

2 (1-ounce) squares unsweetened
    chocolate

2 eggs

1 cup sugar

¾ cup all-purpose flour

1 teaspoon vanilla

Mint chocolate chip ice cream
    *or* other ice cream

Fudge ice cream topping, warmed

❶ Heat margarine or butter and chocolate in medium saucepan over low heat, stirring until chocolate melts. Remove from heat. Cool slightly.

❷ Stir in eggs, sugar, flour and vanilla. Pour mixture into greased and floured 9-inch pie plate.

❸ Bake in preheated 350°F oven about 30 minutes or until a slight imprint remains when touched in center. Cool at room temperature for 30 minutes.

❹ Top pie wedges with ice cream; drizzle with warm topping. Serve immediately.

# Oreo Cheesecake

MAKES 12 SERVINGS • PREP TIME: 25 MINUTES
COOK TIME: 50 MINUTES • COOL TIME: 1 HOUR
CHILL TIME: 4 HOURS

1 (1-pound 4-ounce) package OREO Chocolate Sandwich Cookies, divided

¼ cup margarine *or* butter, melted

2 (8-ounce) packages cream cheese, softened

¾ cup sugar

3 eggs

1 (16-ounce) container dairy sour cream

1 teaspoon vanilla extract

❶ Reserve 6 cookies for garnish. Finely crush *half* of the remaining cookies. Coarsely chop the remaining half of cookies; set aside.

❷ Mix finely crushed cookie crumbs and margarine or butter in bowl. Press onto bottom and 1½ inches up side of a 9-inch springform pan; set aside.

❸ Beat cream cheese and sugar in large bowl with electric mixer at medium speed until creamy. Beat in eggs, sour cream and vanilla at low speed. Fold in coarsely chopped cookies. Spread mixture into prepared crust.

❹ Bake in preheated 350°F oven for 50 to 60 minutes or until set. Cool at room temperature for 1 hour. Cover and refrigerate for at least 4 hours.

❺ Remove side of pan. Halve reserved cookies. Garnish cheesecake with cookie halves.

**OREO CHEESECAKE**

# Oreo Mud Pie

26 OREO Chocolate Sandwich
  Cookies, divided
3 tablespoons margarine *or*
  butter, melted
1 pint chocolate ice cream, softened

1 pint coffee ice cream, softened
½ cup heavy cream, whipped
¼ cup PLANTERS Walnuts, chopped
  and toasted
½ cup fudge ice cream topping

❶ Finely crush 12 cookies; mix with margarine or butter in bowl. Press onto bottom of 9-inch pie plate. Stand remaining cookies around edge of pie plate. Freeze for 10 minutes.

❷ Carefully spread chocolate ice cream into prepared crust. Scoop coffee ice cream with a small ice cream scoop, arranging scoops in a single layer over chocolate layer. Cover and freeze for 4 hours or until firm.

❸ Top pie with whipped cream, walnuts and fudge ice cream topping. Serve immediately.

### CAUTION WITH CUSTARDS

*For custards such as Crème Brûlée (at right), whisk the hot cream, little by little, into the beaten egg yolks so they warm gradually. (If the hot liquid is added all at once, it begins to cook the yolks, creating lumps of cooked egg.) To guard against uneven cooking in the oven, place custard cups in a baking pan and carefully pour boiling water around them. The boiling water serves as a buffer that transfers the heat evenly.*

# Mock Crème Brûlée

2 cups half-and-half *or* light cream

5 egg yolks, slightly beaten

⅓ cup sugar

1 teaspoon vanilla

⅛ teaspoon salt

⅓ cup caramel ice cream topping

Half-and-half *or* light cream, optional

❶ Heat 2 cups half-and-half or light cream in small saucepan over medium heat just to a boil. Remove from heat; set aside.

❷ Mix egg yolks, sugar, vanilla and salt in bowl. Beat with a wire whisk or rotary beater just until combined. Slowly whisk in hot half-and-half or light cream.

❸ Place 6 (¾-cup) soufflé dishes or 6 (6-ounce) custard cups in a 13x9x2-inch baking pan. Set pan on oven rack. Pour custard mixture evenly into dishes or cups. Pour enough boiling water into baking pan around dishes to reach halfway up sides of dishes.

❹ Bake in preheated 325°F oven for 35 to 40 minutes or until a knife inserted near center of each custard comes out clean. Remove custards from water. Cool at room temperature for 1 hour. Cover and refrigerate for at least 1 hour or up to 8 hours.

❺ Let stand at room temperature for 20 minutes before serving. Thin topping with additional half-and-half or light cream, if desired. Drizzle topping over custards.

# Whiskey-Sauced Bread Pudding

**MAKES 6 SERVINGS • PREP TIME: 15 MINUTES**
**COOK TIME: 40 MINUTES**

4 cups cinnamon-swirl *or*
 cinnamon-raisin-swirl bread
 cut into 1-inch cubes (about
 5 to 6 slices)
4 eggs, beaten

1¾ cups milk
⅓ cup sugar
 3 tablespoons bourbon *or* milk, divided
½ cup caramel ice cream topping

❶ Place bread cubes in greased 2-quart square baking dish.

❷ Mix eggs, milk, sugar and 2 tablespoons bourbon or milk in bowl. Pour over bread cubes; press lightly with back of spoon to completely coat bread cubes with egg mixture.

❸ Bake in preheated 350°F oven for 40 to 45 minutes or until a knife inserted near center comes out clean. Cool slightly.

❹ Heat caramel topping and remaining bourbon or milk in small saucepan over medium-low heat until warm. Serve bourbon sauce over warm bread pudding.

# Bananas Foster

**MAKES 4 SERVINGS • PREP TIME: 10 MINUTES**
**COOK TIME: 8 MINUTES**

⅓ cup margarine *or* butter
⅓ cup packed brown sugar
3 ripe bananas, bias sliced
 (about 2 cups)

¼ teaspoon ground cinnamon
2 tablespoons crème de cacao
 *or* banana liqueur
¼ cup rum
 Rich vanilla ice cream

❶ Heat margarine or butter and brown sugar in large skillet over medium heat until melted. Add bananas; cook and gently stir about 2 minutes or until heated through. Sprinkle with cinnamon. Stir in crème de cacao or banana liqueur.

❷ Heat rum in small saucepan over low heat until it almost simmers. Carefully ignite rum; pour over bananas. Serve immediately with ice cream.

# Old-Fashioned Rice Pudding

MAKES 5 SERVINGS • PREP TIME: 10 MINUTES
COOK TIME: 30 MINUTES

2 cups half-and-half *or* light cream
⅓ cup long-grain rice
⅓ cup sugar
3 eggs, beaten

⅓ cup seedless golden raisins
1 teaspoon vanilla extract
¼ teaspoon ground cinnamon

❶ Heat half-and-half or light cream in heavy medium saucepan over medium heat just to a boil. Stir in rice and sugar; return to a boil. Reduce heat; cover and simmer for 20 minutes, stirring occasionally, or until rice is tender.

❷ Stir about 1 cup of the rice mixture into beaten eggs; slowly stir egg mixture back into rice mixture in saucepan.

❸ Cook and stir over medium heat about 3 minutes or until slightly thickened (do not boil). Remove from heat. Stir in raisins, vanilla and cinnamon. Place saucepan over ice cubes for 2 minutes, stirring pudding constantly.

❹ Spoon pudding into a serving bowl or 5 individual dessert dishes. Serve warm or cover and refrigerate until serving time.

### THE PROOF IS IN THE PUDDING

*To test the stage of doneness of a baked pudding or custard, insert a table knife about 1 inch from the middle of the mixture. If no liquid clings to the knife when you withdraw it, the pudding is ready to remove from the oven.*

APPLES 'N' CREAM PIE

# Apples 'n' Cream Pie

**MAKES 8 SERVINGS • PREP TIME: 25 MINUTES**
**COOK TIME: 45 MINUTES • COOL TIME: 1 HOUR**

1 (15-ounce) package folded
    refrigerated unbaked piecrusts
5 cups sliced, peeled baking apples
    (about 5 medium)
1 cup sugar

¼ cup all-purpose flour
½ teaspoon apple pie spice
⅔ cup half-and-half *or* light cream

❶ Place 1 piecrust in a 9-inch pie plate according to package directions.

❷ Place apples in the lined plate. Mix sugar, flour and spice in medium bowl. Stir in half-and-half or light cream. Pour over apples. Cut slits in top crust. Place top crust on filling. Fold top crust under bottom crust; flute edge.

❸ Cover edge of crust with foil. Bake in preheated 375°F oven for 25 minutes. Remove foil. Brush crust with additional half-and-half or light cream, if desired. Bake for 20 to 25 minutes more or until top is golden and apples are tender. Let stand at room temperature for at least 1 hour. Serve warm.

---

### PICKING THE PERFECT PIE APPLE

*The apple of your eye isn't necessarily the one for your pie. Apple varieties differ in texture and sweetness. For a sweet pie apple, try Cortland, Crispin, Criterion, Fuji, Golden Delicious or Jonagold apples. For a slight tart flavor, choose Jonathan, Rome Beauty, Newtown Pippin, Stayman or York Imperial. Or, if you like a more pronounced tart taste, opt for Granny Smith apples.*

# Index

# Index

### TIPS

# Metric Cooking Hints

By making a few conversions, cooks in Australia, Canada, and the United Kingdom can use these recipes with confidence. The charts on this page provide a guide for converting measurements from the U.S. customary system, which is used throughout this book, to the imperial and metric systems. There also is a conversion table for oven temperatures to accommodate the differences in oven calibrations.

**Product Differences:** Most of the ingredients called for in the recipes in this book are available in English-speaking countries. However, some are known by different names. Here are some common American ingredients and their possible counterparts:
- Sugar is granulated or castor sugar.
- Powdered sugar is icing sugar.
- All-purpose flour is plain household flour or white flour. When self-rising flour is used in place of all-purpose flour in a recipe that calls for leavening, omit the leavening agent (baking soda or baking powder) and salt.
- Light-colored corn syrup is golden syrup.
- Cornstarch is cornflour.
- Baking soda is bicarbonate of soda.
- Vanilla is vanilla essence.
- Green, red, or yellow bell peppers are capsicums.
- Golden raisins are sultanas.

**Volume and Weight:** Americans traditionally use cup measures for liquid and solid ingredients. The chart, above right, shows the approximate imperial and metric equivalents. If you are accustomed to weighing solid ingredients, the following approximate equivalents will be helpful.
- 1 cup butter, castor sugar, or rice = 8 ounces = about 250 grams
- 1 cup flour = 4 ounces = about 125 grams
- 1 cup icing sugar = 5 ounces = about 150 grams

Spoon measures are used for smaller amounts of ingredients. Although the size of the tablespoon varies slightly in different countries, for practical purposes and for recipes in this book, a straight substitution is all that's necessary.

Measurements made using cups or spoons always should be level unless stated otherwise.

# Equivalents: U.S. = Australia/U.K.

⅛ teaspoon = 0.5 ml
¼ teaspoon = 1 ml
½ teaspoon = 2 ml
1 teaspoon = 5 ml
1 tablespoon = 1 tablespoon
¼ cup = 2 tablespoons = 2 fluid ounces = 60 ml
⅓ cup = ¼ cup = 3 fluid ounces = 90 ml
½ cup = ⅓ cup = 4 fluid ounces = 120 ml
⅔ cup = ½ cup = 5 fluid ounces = 150 ml
¾ cup = ⅔ cup = 6 fluid ounces = 180 ml
1 cup = ¾ cup = 8 fluid ounces = 240 ml
1¼ cups = 1 cup
2 cups = 1 pint
1 quart = 1 liter
½ inch = 1.27 cm
1 inch = 2.54 cm

## Baking Pan Sizes

| American | Metric |
|---|---|
| 8×1½-inch round baking pan | 20×4-cm cake tin |
| 9×1½-inch round baking pan | 23×3.5-cm cake tin |
| 11×7×1½-inch baking pan | 28×18×4-cm baking tin |
| 13×9×2-inch baking pan | 30×20×3-cm baking tin |
| 2-quart rectangular baking dish | 30×20×3-cm baking tin |
| 15×10×1-inch baking pan | 30×25×2-cm baking tin (Swiss roll tin) |
| 9-inch pie plate | 22×4- or 23×4-cm pie plate |
| 7- or 8-inch springform pan | 18- or 20-cm springform or loose-bottom cake tin |
| 9×5×3-inch loaf pan | 23×13×7-cm or 2-pound narrow loaf tin or pâté tin |
| 1½-quart casserole | 1.5-liter casserole |

## Oven Temperature Equivalents

| Fahrenheit Setting | Celsius Setting* | Gas Setting |
|---|---|---|
| 300°F | 150°C | Gas Mark 2 (slow) |
| 325°F | 160°C | Gas Mark 3 (moderately slow) |
| 350°F | 180°C | Gas Mark 4 (moderate) |
| 375°F | 190°C | Gas Mark 5 (moderately hot) |
| 400°F | 200°C | Gas Mark 6 (hot) |
| 425°F | 220°C | Gas Mark 7 |
| 450°F | 230°C | Gas Mark 8 (very hot) |
| Broil | | Grill |

*Electric and gas ovens may be calibrated using Celsius. However, for an electric oven, increase the Celsius setting 10 to 20 degrees when cooking above 160°C. For convection or forced-air ovens (gas or electric), lower the temperature setting 10°C when cooking at all heat levels.